The Usborne
Book of
Silly
Jokes

D1372546

DESIGNED AND ILLUSTRATED BY LEONARD LE ROLLAND
EDITED BY LAURA HOWELL

CONTENTS

AROUND THE WORLD   5

A jet-setting joke journey.

GHASTLY GAGS   19

Ghosts, gremlins and ghoulish guffaws.

CLASSIC JOKES   35

Worth crossing the road for.

DANGER! WILD ANIMALS   49

These jokes might drive you wild too!

FUNNY BUSINESS   65

Having a job isn't all hard work...

EVERYDAY LAUGHS   81

The funny side of life.

AROUND THE WORLD

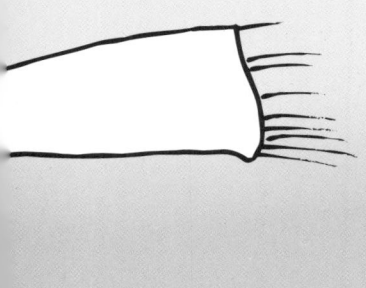

Down under

What's Australia's most popular drink?
Coca-Koala.

What's the scariest part of Australia?
The Northern Terror-tory.

How do you describe an
exhausted kangaroo?
Out of bounds.

What do you call a boomerang
that doesn't come back?
A stick.

What famous story was about an
Australian reptile?
The Lizard of Oz.

Why do mother koalas carry their babies?
**Because the babies are too small to carry
the mothers.**

What do you get if you cross a kangaroo
with an elephant?
Huge potholes all over Australia.

What's purple and furry?
A kangaroo holding its breath.

North America

What is white, furry and found in Florida?
A polar bear with a bad sense of direction.

What American city do cows live in?
Moo York.

Knock knock.

Who's there?

Alaska.

Alaska who?

Alaska again, will you please open the door?

What is the capital of Canada?
C.

Where do you find Quebec?
On a map.

What holiday do American vampires celebrate?
Fangsgiving.

What stands in New York and sneezes all day?
The a-choo of Liberty.

What would you get if you crossed a
gorilla with an American president?
Ape-raham Lincoln.

Who was America's first animated president?
George Washingtoon.

Europe

Why is Europe like a frying pan?
Because it has Greece at the bottom.

Why did the Irishman go to the foot doctor?
He had lepre-corns.

How do you make a Venetian blind?
Poke him in the eye.

What's tall, Italian and covered in pepperoni?
The leaning tower of Pizza.

Why should you be worried if you eat bad
food in Germany?
Because the wurst is yet to come.

dot

dot dash

What happened to the Frenchman who fell into the river in Paris?

He was declared in-Seine.

Where's the best place in Europe to find sharks?

Finland.

What does a Spanish farmer say to his hens?

Olé!

Where was the Queen of England crowned?

On her head.

How did Vikings send secret messages?

By Norse code.

dot dot

dash

Out of this world

What kind of music can you hear in space?
A Nep-tune.

What sea is in space?
The galax-sea.

How do you get a baby astronaut to sleep?
Rocket.

What do you call a wizard in outer space?
A flying sorcerer.

Where do astronauts leave their spaceships?
At parking meteors.

All at sea

What can fly underwater?
A parrot in a submarine.

What's the best way to
communicate with a fish?
Drop it a line.

How do fish get to school?
By octobus.

What do you call a stupid squid?
A squidiot.

Why are goldfish orange?

Because the water
turns us rusty.

Why did the fish take an aspirin?
Because it had a haddock.

What sits on the
seabed and shakes?
A nervous wreck.

What kind of fish
only swims at night?
A starfish.

All over the place

What do you say if someone tells a lie in South America?

I don't Bolivia.

Why do Egyptian pyramids have doorbells?

So you can toot-'n'-come-in.

What do you find in the middle of Japan?

The letter "p".

How would you describe the rain in Spain?

Little drops of water falling from the sky.

17

There was a young zombie named Khan,
Who was known for his kindness and charm.
If a stranger or friend
Ever needed a hand,
He'd give them a leg or an arm.

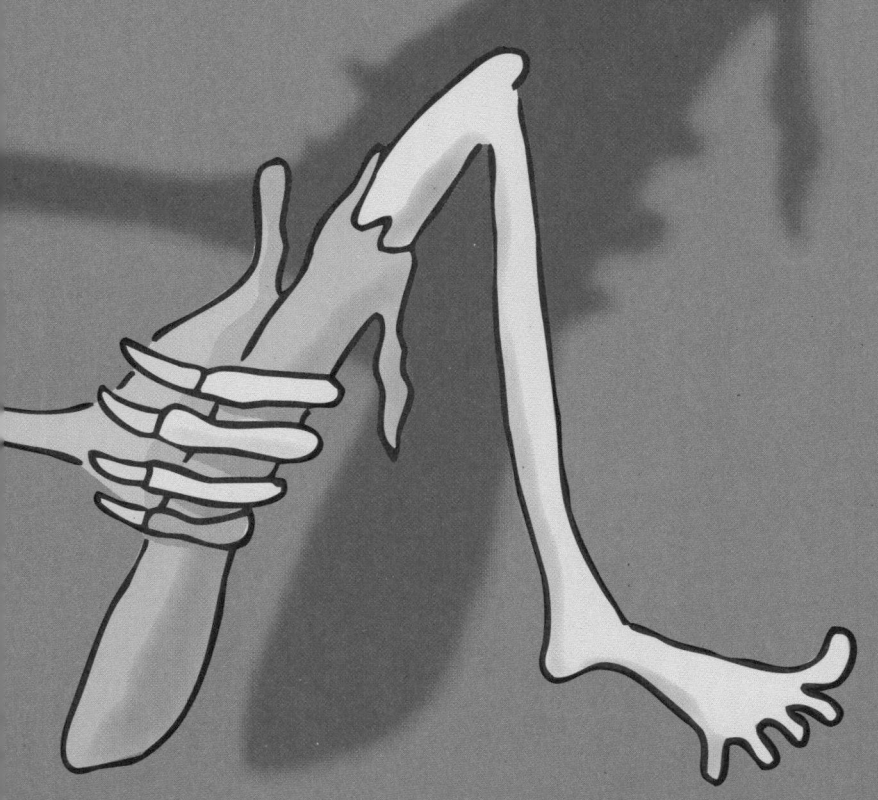

GHASTLY GAGS

Fang-tastic!

What movie do vampires like best?
Batman.

What kind of coffee does Dracula drink?
Decoffinated.

What kind of mail does a famous vampire get?
Fang mail.

Who did Dracula get engaged to?
His girl-fiend.

What do you get if you meet Dracula in the middle of winter?
Frostbite.

What happened to the vampires who wanted to make a movie?
They couldn't find a good crypt writer.

What kind of jewels do vampires wear?
Tomb stones.

Why do people hate being bitten by vampires?
Because it's a drain in the neck.

What does a vampire bathe in?
A bat tub.

Why are vampires like false teeth?
They come out at night.

Hairy and scary

What does a werewolf write at the end of a letter?
"Best vicious"

Why did the werewolf buy two tickets at the zoo?
One to get in and one to get out.

What do you call a dentist who treats werewolves?
Brave.

What happened when the werewolf swallowed a clock?

He got ticks.

What did the zombie get a medal for?
Deadication.

What does a little zombie call his parents?
Mummy and Deady.

What do you call twin zombies in a belfry?
Dead ringers.

Where do zombies go on vacation?
The Deaditerranean.

Why did the doctor tell the zombie to take a rest?

He was dead on his feet.

Frankie panky

Why did Frankenstein's monster get indigestion?

He bolted down his food.

What happened when Frankenstein's monster swallowed some plutonium?

He got atomic ache.

I heard Dr. Frankenstein is going to marry the invisible woman.

I don't know what he sees in her.

What should you do if you find yourself surrounded by Frankenstein's monster, Count Dracula and the wolfman?

Hope you're at a Halloween party.

What was written on Frankenstein's monster's grave?
"Rust in peace"

Why was Dr. Frankenstein never lonely?
He was good at making friends.

What do you call a clever monster?
Frank Einstein.

What did Frankenstein's monster say to the screwdriver?
"Daddy!"

What's the best way to speak to Frankenstein's monster?
From a distance.

Ghoulish giggles

Who protects the shores where ghosts live?
The ghost guard.

When does a ghost eat breakfast?
In the moaning.

What do you get when you cross Bambi with a ghost?
Bam-boo.

What do you call a ghost's mother and father?
Trans-parents.

When do ghosts usually appear?
Just before someone screams.

Who's the world's most famous ghost detective?
Sherlock Moans.

Hag gags

Why do witches buy magazines?
They like to read the horrorscopes.

What happened to the naughty little witch
at school?
She was ex-spelled.

What do you call a witch who drives really badly?
A road hag.

What do you call an old hag who lives by the sea?
A sandwitch.

Who went into a witch's den and came out alive?
The witch.

How do you know a witch is really ugly?
When a wasp stings her, it closes its eyes.

What do you call a witch with one leg?
Eileen.

Why do witches only ride their
broomsticks after dark?
That's the time to go to sweep.

What do witches put on their hair?
Scare spray.

What did the witch do when her broomstick broke?
She witch-hiked.

What does a witch ask for when she's in a hotel?
Broom service.

Funny bones

Why don't skeletons play music in church?

They have no organs.

What happened to the skeleton who was attacked by a dog?

He didn't have a leg to stand on.

Why do you have to wait so long for a ghost train?

Because they only run a skeleton service.

How do you describe a lazy skeleton?

Bone idle.

What do skeletons say before they start to eat?

Bone appetit.

Why did the skeleton go to the
Chinese restaurant?
To buy some spare ribs.

Why didn't the skeleton go skydiving?
He didn't have the guts.

Who was the most famous French skeleton?
Napoleon Bone-apart.

How do skeletons
call their friends?

On the telebone.

M-m-monsters!

What does a polite monster say when he meets you for the first time?
Pleased to eat you!

When are monsters most likely to eat people?
On Chewsday.

How do you know if a monster has a glass eye?
When it comes out in conversation.

Did you hear about the monster who had eight arms?
He said they came in handy.

Where are yetis found?
They're so big, they're hardly ever lost.

How does a yeti get to work?
By icicle.

What do you do with a blue monster?
Try to cheer him up.

Why did the bride of Frankenstein get squeezed to death?
He had a crush on her.

What do you call a monster with 100 children?
Dad.

If a stork brings human babies, what brings monster babies?
A crane.

An Italian girl known as Mona,
Told jokes that would make
people groan-a.
Though the gags made her smile,
Her friends ran a mile
And she ended up laughing alone-a.

Classic Jokes

What do you get if you cross...

... a rabbit with a kettle?

A hot cross bunny.

... a hen with a guitar?

A chicken that plucks itself.

... a barber with a ghost?

A scare-dresser.

... a frog with a chair?

A toadstool.

... a skunk with a fairy?

Stinkerbell.

... an artist with a policeman?

A brush with the law.

... a computer with a banana skin?
A slipped disk.

... a snowman with a witch?
A cold spell.

... a big ape with a plane?
King Kongcorde.

... a muppet with a tree?
Kermit the log.

... a lake with a leaky boat?

About halfway.

What's the difference...

... between an oak tree and a tight shoe?
One make acorns, the other makes corns ache.

... between a hungry man and a greedy man?
One longs to eat and the other eats too long.

... between a fly and a bird?
A bird can fly, but a fly can't bird.

... between apples and elephant dung?

I don't know.

I'm never going to ask you to bake a pie, then.

... between a crazy dog and a short-sighted teacher?
One barks madly and the other marks badly.

... between a big hill and a big pill?
One's hard to get up, the other's hard to get down.

... between an overweight person and a bored guest?
One's going to diet and the other's dying to go.

What do you call...

... a girl who stands in the middle of a tennis court?

Annette.

... a boy with a seagull on his head?

Cliff.

... a boy who floats in the sea?

Bob.

... a man who stops a river?

Adam.

... a deer with no eyes?

No idea.

... a deer with no eyes or legs?

Still no idea.

... two men who hang over a window?

Kurt 'n' Rod.

... a man who sits near a door?
Matt.

... a man with a shovel on his head?
Doug.

... a boy with a paper bag on his head?
Russell.

... a man with a car on his head?
Jack.

... a man with a bus on his head?
The deceased.

Knock knock!

Knock knock.

Who's there?

Dishwasher.

Dishwasher who?

Dishwasher way I shpoke when I losht my falsh teef.

Knock knock.

Who's there?

Lettuce.

Lettuce who?

Lettuce in and I'll tell you.

Knock knock.

Who's there?

Ammonia.

Ammonia who?

Ammonia little boy, I can't reach the doorbell.

43

45

Crossing the road

Why did the cow cross the road?
To get to the udder side.

Why did the vampire cross the road?
To get to the blood bank.

Why did the chicken cross the building site?
She wanted to see a man laying bricks.

Why did the elephant cross the road?

It was the chicken's day off.

Why did the chicken cross the road, roll in a muddy puddle and cross the road again?
Because she was a dirty double-crosser.

Why did the whale cross the ocean?

To get to the other tide.

Why did the birdwatcher cross the road?

To get to the other hide.

Why did the wasp cross the road?

To get to the waspital.

Why did the orange only get halfway across the road?

It ran out of juice.

Why did the turkey cross the road?

To prove he wasn't chicken.

DANGER!

WILD ANIMALS

ENTER AT OWN RISK

Crazy critters

How did the pig get to the hospital?

In a hambulance.

Why did the ram run over the cliff?

He didn't see the ewe turn.

What do you call a sleeping bull?

A bulldozer.

What do you give a sick frog?

A hoperation.

What do you give an elephant with an upset stomach?

Plenty of room.

Where would you find a tortoise with no legs?
Where you left it.

What sort of fish would you find in a bird cage?
A perch.

Where do rabbits go when they get married?
On their bunnymoon.

What's the largest kind of ant in the world?
An elephant.

What do you call
a dead skunk?

Ex-stinkt.

Where do anteaters like to eat?

In a restaur-ant.

What does a snake write at the end of a letter?

Love and hisses.

How do you stop a rhino from charging?

Take away its credit cards.

Where do baby gorillas sleep?

In ape-ri-cots.

What do you get if you cross a parrot with a centipede?

A walkie-talkie.

Down on the farm

What do you call a tall building that's full of pigs?
A sty-scraper.

How do you hire a horse?
Put it on stilts.

How many sheep does it take
to make a sweater?
None, sheep can't knit.

What goes "aaab-aaab"?
A sheep in reverse.

What's the best cure for chicken pox?
Henicillin.

What do you get if you cross a cow with an octopus?
An animal that milks itself.

Did you hear about the tractor with the wooden wheels and the wooden engine?
It wooden go.

What does a pig use to write letters?
A pen and oink.

What game do horses like to play?
Stable tennis.

What has feathers and haunts the farmyard?
A goost.

How do sheep keep warm in winter?

Central bleating.

Why did the foal cough?
Because it was a little hoarse.

Feline funnies

What do cats like to read every morning?

The daily mewspaper.

What kind of cats do you find in Poland?

Pole-cats.

Where do hungry cats go in summer?

The Canary Islands.

What type of cats are like a chain?

Lynx.

What kind of paintings can cats do best?

Paw-traits.

What do you get when you cross a cat with a tree?

A cat-a-log.

What kind of food do Chinese cats like to eat?

Egg fried mice.

What do you get if you cross a cat with a bat?

A cat flap.

What do you get if you cross a tomcat with a Pekingese?

A Peking Tom.

What do you call an upper-class feline?

An aristocat.

It's a dog's life

Which side of a dog has the most fur?

The outside.

What kind of dog has no head, no legs and no tail?

A hot dog.

What do you call a dog who travels around the world?

A jet-setter.

Why did the dog put her puppies in a box?

Because you shouldn't leave your litter lying around.

What type of dog has the cleanest fur?

A shampoodle.

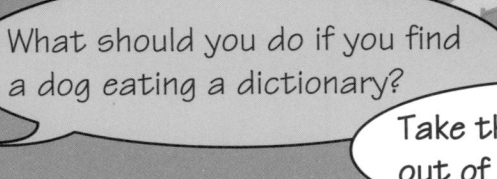

What should you do if you find a dog eating a dictionary?

Take the words right out of its mouth.

What dog is always in a hurry?

A Dash-hund.

Why are dogs' noses cold and wet?

Because no one ever offers them a tissue.

What happened when the dog went to the flea circus?

He stole the show.

Birdbrained

What do you call a crate full of ducks?

A box of quackers.

What does a penguin have that no other bird has?

Baby penguins.

What bird can be heard at mealtimes?

A swallow.

What subject are owls best at in school?

Owlgebra.

What's green and jumps out of planes with a gun?
A parrot-trooper.

What do birds like to watch after the News?
The feather forecast.

What goes "quick quick"?
A duck with hiccups.

Creepy crawlies

Did you hear about the two silkworms who had a race?

It ended in a tie.

What did the flea say to the other flea?

Shall we walk or take the cat?

What's the world's largest moth?

A mam-moth.

What flies, has stripes and is very clumsy?

A fumble bee.

How do you tell which end of a worm is which?

Tickle the middle and see which end laughs.

How do you describe a very cold flea?
Flea-zing.

What do bees say when they get back from work?

Honey, I'm home.

What did the priest say when he saw a fly?
Let us spray.

Did you hear about the smart leech?
He was no sucker.

If bees make honey, what do wasps make?

Waspberry jam.

Funny Business

Making a living

Why did the baker stop making donuts?
He was sick of the hole business.

What's purple and fixes pipes?
A plum-er.

What's the difference between a night watchman and a butcher?
One stays awake, the other weighs a steak.

Did you hear about the plastic surgeon?
He stood in front of a fire and melted.

Why are goalkeepers always at the bank?
Because they're good savers.

Did you hear about the undertaker who buried a person in the wrong place?
It was a grave error.

Optician: Have your eyes ever been checked?
Customer: No, always plain blue.

I'm learning to be a barber.

Is it taking long?

No, I'm studying all the short cuts.

Barber: How would you like your hair cut?
Customer: Shorter, please.

What did the actor say when the trapdoor opened?
Don't worry, it's just a stage I'm going through.

If athletes get athlete's foot, what do rocket scientists get?
Missile-toe.

Work, work, work...

How does a farmer count his cows?

With a cowculator.

What music do florists listen to?

Heavy petal.

Who wears a crown and climbs ladders?

A window queen-er.

What does an artist do just before he dies?

Draws his last breath.

What does a musician do with her old sheet music?

Puts it on the compose heap.

Why are dentists so miserable?

Because they're always looking down in the mouth.

How do you make a bandstand?

Take their chairs away.

Where do firefighters go when they get hurt?

To a hose-pital.

What's the best time to visit the dentist?

Tooth-hurty.

Did you hear about the dishonest butcher?

He was caught choplifting.

Waiter, waiter!

Waiter, this coffee tastes like mud.

I'm not surprised, it was ground this morning.

Waiter, this soup tastes funny!

Why aren't you laughing then?

Waiter, this egg is bad.

Don't blame me, I only laid the table.

Waiter, what's this in my salad?

I really couldn't say, sir. All bugs look the same to me.

Waiter, I can't eat this disgusting food.
Get the manager.
It's no use, ma'am, he won't eat it either.

Waiter, waiter! My water's cloudy.
You're mistaken, ma'am. That's the dirt on the glass.

Waiter, this cheese is full of holes.
It could be worse, sir. It used to be full of maggots.

Waiter, will my pizza be long?

No sir, it'll be round.

Cops and robbers

What does a policeman use to tell you the time?
A crime watch.

What happened to the burglar who broke into a calendar factory?
He got twelve months.

What happened to the burglar who fell into a cement mixer?
He became a hardened criminal.

Why did the thief saw the legs off his bed?
He wanted to lie low.

Why was the photographer arrested?
The police found his prints at the scene of a crime.

Did you hear about the man who was arrested for selling self-portraits?
He was framed.

Why are police officers so strong?
Because they hold up traffic.

What happened to the robber who stole a lamp?
He got a light sentence.

Why do criminals shower so often?
They like to make a clean getaway.

Silly sports

Why are babies fast swimmers?
Because they're good at the crawl.

What do you call a bird at the end of
a marathon?
Puffin.

Why are baseball fields so valuable?
Because they have a diamond in the middle.

What country do jockeys come from?
Horse-tralia.

What drink do soccer players like least?
Penal-tea.

Why didn't the two elephants enter
the swimming race?
**They only had one pair of trunks
between them.**

What drink do boxers like best?
Punch.

What happened to the soccer player whose eyesight began to fail?
He became a referee.

Doctor, doctor!

Doctor, doctor! I've just swallowed a pen.
What should I do?
Oh, don't worry. Just use a pencil.

Doctor, doctor, I feel like an ice cream cone.
Me too — I think I'll go out and buy one.

Doctor, doctor, will you take my temperature?
No need, I have one of my own.

Doctor, doctor, I feel like a clock.

You're too wound up.

77

Shiver me timbers!

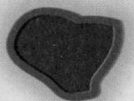

What do you call a pirate who makes lots of mistakes?
Wrong John Silver.

Where do you take a sick pirate ship?
To the dock.

What toys do pirates' children like to play with?
Yo-ho-ho-yos.

How do you make a pirate angry?
Take away the "p" and he becomes irate.

Why couldn't the pirates play cards?
The captain was standing on the deck.

Why did the pirate have twigs in his beard?
He'd been sleeping in the crow's nest.

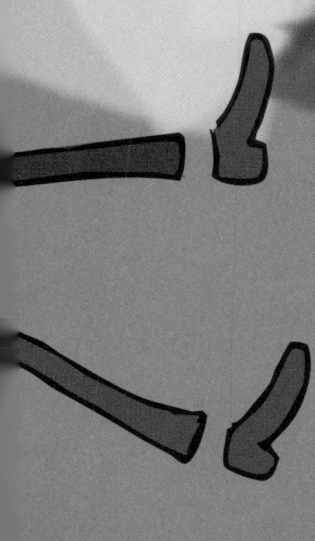

Everyday Laughs

Parents!

My mother just had a new baby.

Why, what was wrong with the old one?

Do you think our son gets his brains from me?

Probably, dear. I still have all of mine.

Daddy, there's a man with a beard at the door.

Tell him I've got one already.

Did you hear about the carpenter's son?

He's a chip off the old block.

I'll teach you to throw stones at my greenhouse!

I wish you would, Dad. I've had ten shots and haven't hit it once.

What did you get for Christmas?

A harmonica. It's the best present I've ever had.

Why?

My mother pays me not to play it.

Jimmy, did you take a bath?

Why, is one missing?

Can I have a new pair of shoes, Dad?

Of course, son. As soon as your brother's grown out of them.

Silly siblings

I just got a puppy for my little brother.

Sounds like a fair trade.

Why is your sister so short?

She's my half-sister.

Sis, are caterpillars good to eat?

Of course not! Why do you ask?

There was one on your salad, but it's gone now.

My little brother's a real pain.

It could be worse. He could be twins.

Classroom capers

87

Hilarious holidays

What is Santa's wife called?

Mary Christmas.

Where does Valentine's day come after Easter?

In the dictionary.

Why do we paint Easter eggs?

It's easier than trying to wallpaper them.

What monster plays the most April Fool's jokes?

Prankenstein.

What do canaries do on Halloween night?

They go trick or tweeting.

What do the elves sing to Santa on his birthday?

"Freeze a jolly good fellow..."

Who delivers presents to baby sharks at Christmas?

Santa Jaws.

What did the painter say to his girlfriend on Valentine's day?

I love you with all my art.

A feast of fun

Why do lions eat raw meat?

Have you ever tried to teach one to cook?

Should you stir your coffee with your left hand or your right?

Neither, you should use a spoon.

Why did the tomato turn red?

Because it saw the salad dressing.

What did the hungry computer eat?

Chips, one byte at a time.

What's yellow and fills
fields with music? Pop-corn.

What did one plate say
to the other?
Lunch is on me.

What's round, white
and giggles? A tickled onion.

What's worse than finding
a maggot in your apple?
Finding half a maggot.

Getting around

What flies and smells bad?

A smellycopter.

Where can you buy a cheap yacht?

In a sail.

How do lobsters get to work?

In a taxi crab.

How do fleas travel?

They itch-hike.

How do you know that planes are afraid of the dark?

They have to leave the landing lights on.

What do you call a stupid boat?
An idi-yacht.

What did the traffic lights say to the traffic?
Don't peek, I'm changing.

What form of transport do carpenters prefer?
Planes!

What sport do flat fish like best?
Skate-boarding.

What happens to broken-down frogs?

They get toad away.

Worn-out jokes

What did the tie say to the hat?

You go on ahead while I hang around.

Did you hear about the boy who put on a clean pair of socks every day?

By the end of the week he couldn't get his shoes on.

How should you dress on a cold day?

Quickly.

What clothing can you make out of two banana skins?

A pair of slippers.

First published in 2003 by Usborne Publishing Ltd.,
Usborne House, 83-85 Saffron Hill, London, EC1N 8RT, England.
www.usborne.com

UE. First published in America 2004.
American editor: Carrie Seay

Printed in Italy